© Copyright 1991 Omnibus Press
(A Division of Book Sales Limited)

Editorial by Mick St Michael
Picture Research by Dave Brolan
Cover designed by Four Corners Design
Book designed by Tim McPhee

ISBN 0.7119.2776.6   Order No. OP 46630

GW00703137

Exclusive distributors:
Book Sales Limited
8/9 Frith Street, London W1V 5TZ, UK.
Music Sales Corporation
257 Park Avenue South, New York, NY 10010, USA.
Music Sales Pty Limited
120 Rothschild Avenue, Rosebery, NSW 2018, Australia.
To the Music Trade only:
Music Sales Limited
8/9 Frith Street, London W1V 5TZ, UK.

Typeset by Cambridge Photosetting Services
Design and separation in association with
Book Production Consultants, Cambridge
Printed in Great Britain by Ebenezer Baylis Ltd, Worcester
Photographs supplied by LFI, Barry Plummer,
SIN (Kata Natola), Kevin Williams,
Justin Thomas/All Action, Gene Kirkland/Retna
Every effort has been made to trace the copyright
holders of the photographs in this book but one or two
were unreachable. We would be grateful if the photographers
concerned would contact us.
A catalogue record for this book is available from
the British Library.

OMNIBUS PRESS
LONDON · NEW YORK · SYDNEY

GUNS N' ROSES

In the Sixties, The Rolling Stones won the accolade of the World's Greatest Rock'n'Roll Band – and lived it to the full. They and they alone marked the generation gap: love them or hate them, no-one could sit on the fence. The Stones still roll (just) in the Nineties – but the banner they once flew has been crucially modified by the group that proudly carries it now. They're Guns N'Roses – and they're the Most Dangerous Band in the World!

Loud, proud and dirty, their first album's cover was banned by the chainstores . . . its home-made predecessor had a title no music paper would dare print in full. They topped the chart with just their third single. They kept the world waiting four years for their second (proper) album – but got away with it. At least three of the line-up have admitted to dicing with a drug-induced demise. But they kept their balance, stayed on the tightrope and in doing so wrote their names large in rock legend.

The seeds of Guns N'Roses success were sown way back in 1979 when Slash and Steven Adler, then just 14 years of age, first got together to listen and play along to Kiss records in their suburban Los Angeles neighbourhood. (Ironically, Kiss's Paul Stanley was one of the first to pick up on the unsigned band several years later, but the time and place weren't *quite* right.)

Steven had the guitar back then, Slash figuring he might do better with a bass. Even then, though, his luck was out: he describes his first guitar, picked up in a garage sale, as "a one-string plank".

Christened Saul Hudson (a name he hated from childhood), Slash was born in Stoke, England, in 1965 but his American parents soon relocated to the US West Coast. His mother and father were both in the music business as a costumier and record sleeve designer respectively, so he found himself exposed to many different influences. But he found his major inspiration on a date with a girlfriend – when she put 'Aerosmith's Rocks' on the turntable, thoughts of romance receded to the back of his adolescent mind.

Steve Adler was a wild child, born in Cleveland, Ohio, in 1965 but well and truly raised a Hollywood brat. His school career ended abruptly when he dropped out in tenth grade – and to hear his childhood memories, it's surprising he lasted *that* long! "The first time I got wasted I was eight years old," he boasts. "I was in my grandmother's bathroom and I smoked a joint."

He left home for the first time at 12 to stay with the grandma, and though lack of funds kept him from a proper drumkit for the next six years he imitated his idols – Queen's Roger Taylor, The Who's Keith Moon and Led Zeppelin's John Bonham – on biscuit tins and books.

Axl Rose, too, had a torrid childhood. Born in 1962 in downhome Lafayette, Indiana – the kind of insignificant, insular American township you read about in books, where everyone knows everybody else's business – he grew up in total ignorance of his real father, who'd abandoned his mother when their offspring was still rehearsing lead vocals from the crib.

Discovering by chance he wasn't the son of L. Stephen Bailey, the man he'd assumed to have been his natural father, he adopted the name W. Rose instead of the Bill Bailey he'd used all those years. Axl came later from an early Lafayette band he'd sung in, Rose from the man who'd sired him. The initials WAR, we understand, are totally coincidental.

Trouble seemed to find him everywhere . . . even in church, where the Pentecostal choir kicked him out ("I was always getting in trouble for singing everybody else's parts"). He claims to have been thrown in jail over 20 times in his youth for nothing much more than being drunk: when he was wrongly accused of car-stealing, he left town on the next Greyhound.

It looked like his reputation had taken an earlier bus – and, once in Los Angeles, things got worse. "I went out in front of city hall and directed the traffic," he recalls of one drunken binge.

Just like Axl, Izzy Stradlin rebelled against the confines of small-town America where this son of a single- parent family (born 1962) claims "I got drunk . . . cos there was **** all else to do". Significantly, though, Jeff Isabelle (his real name, hence Izzy) was smart enough to wait until after graduation from Lafayette high school before *he* took off. The drums were his first line of escape from suburban boredom, but when he threw his battered kit into the back of an equally decrepit Chevy to try his luck in Los Angeles in 1979 he had no idea how long his adventure would last. As it happens, he's since only been back twice . . .

On arrival in 1979, Izzy's LA lifestyle was far from glamorous. He hustled free meals, busked in subways during the day and struggled on the club circuit at night. His quote "I sold drugs, sold girls, just did what I had to do" has passed into G N'R legend, as has "I've gone five days without eating . . . you just drink water. Sometimes you have no alternative."

But if there's anything worse than starving, it's starving alone. So things had to be changing for the better when at Easter 1980, a knock at the door found a backpacking Axl dripping water on the mat. He'd been tracking down his townmate for the past four weeks, believing LA was about one tenth its actual size!

It *had* to be fate. Two more years of scuffling later, Izzy had mastered the guitar, the duo were writing songs together and writing the first chapter of G N'R legend. Hollywood Rose was born – and though a meal in their cockroach-infested digs consisted of biscuits, gravy and cheap Thunderbird wine, they felt they had a future. One co-conspirator was Chris Weber, who stuck around long enough to co-write 'Anything Goes' on G N'R's first album.

Hollywood Rose bloomed fast and faded faster, merging with bar-band rivals LA Guns to become Guns N'Roses – guitarist Tracii Guns and drummer Rob Gardner supplying the extra manpower. The role of bass player was taken by Duff (real name Michael) McKagan.

Hailing from suburban Seattle where he was born the youngest of eight children in 1964, the fifth man came from something of a musical family: "My brother Bruce started giving me lessons on the bass in eighth grade," he recalls. Switching to drums, he returned to his original instrument in desperation after his kit was trashed by a less than adoring audience. Duff, whose all-time hero is Sid Vicious, yields to no man in his love of English punk/

new wave music, and it's an attitude G N'R have borrowed to tremendous effect.

While Duff's brother instructed him in the gentle art of the four-string bass, his father was educating him in other ways. "My old man gave me some whiskey when I was real young," he recalls. "It was Hawaiian. He said 'Take a swig and pronounce the name.' After about four swigs I couldn't pronounce the name because I was too drunk."

Duff already considered himself a serious musician, having played in at least 30 bands since starting his musical career on the Seattle bar circuit. His first move on

reaching Los Angeles was to answer an ad looking for a bass player "into Alice Cooper and Aerosmith", placed by a pair of local hopefuls. This was his introduction to Roadcrew, the band Steve Adler and Slash were in the process of putting together.

The trio met in an all-night delicatessen, got drunk and got together. But Duff soon discovered that though the duo looked the part, they were somewhat less than dynamic when it came to rehearsing. After six frustrating weeks, he quit to join forces with Axl and Izzy – and when original Guns N'Roses members Guns and Gardner were sacked for displaying less than total dedication, he called his former bandmates. Slash (who'd meanwhile failed the audition for Poison through not being pretty enough!) and Steven seized the opportunity. Weeks of going nowhere had made them leaner, meaner and ready to rehearse until their fingers bled.

The chemistry of the new band was immediately diagnosed as explosive. As one magazine put it, they were "Five different personalities with a single common denominator – cockiness!"

After a 36-hour rehearsal and a debut gig at the Troubadour club, the new Guns N'Roses line-up hit the road on June 1985's 'Hell Tour' . . . which kicked off disastrously when the band's car broke down, forcing them to hitchhike in their stage gear, "striped tight pants and boots," recalls Duff. "When we finally got there we had to play on other people's equipment. It was our first gig and we *sucked* . . . "But if

they could get through that, he concluded "we'd get through *anything*."

They returned to LA to hit the clubs – the Roxy, Whiskey, Troubadour and Scream – and build up their following from the 20 die-hards they'd inherited from the early days of LA Guns to something altogether bigger. Even then, their reputation preceded them: club ads often read 'Fresh From Detox' or 'Addicted – Only The Strong Survive'.

Their early repertoire was padded out with individual interpretations of rock classics like The Rolling Stones' 'Jumpin' Jack Flash' and Elvis's 'Heartbreak Hotel'. A classic of more recent vintage, AC/DC's 'Whole Lotta Rosie', was still in the set when they visited England for the first time.

Guns N'Roses took the LA club circuit by the scruff of the neck and shook until it begged for mercy. Yet despite ecstatic crowd reaction, word had got round the business that these boys were trouble with a capital T.

By no means disheartened by the major labels' lack of guts, Guns N'Roses decided to take the punk route to fame and fortune and released their own record. The label name they chose – Uzi Suicide – matched the logo they'd created of a machine gun and a skull. With expletive mercifully deleted, the EP rejoiced in the title 'Live ?!** Like A Suicide', a handle rivalled only by The Sex Pistols' debut.

By putting their influences on the line, they proved they weren't afraid to stand comparison with the best – in this case

Aerosmith, whose 'Mama Kin' took a good kicking, while lesser-known Australian combo Rose Tattoo contributed 'Nice Boys': the self-penned 'Reckless Life' and 'Move To The City' made up the numbers. The fiery four-tracker only served to increase the buzz already circulating, and suddenly things started to happen.

Vicki Hamilton, talent spotter extraordinary with Poison and Motley Crue to her credit, was the catalyst. "They were definitely outlaws. I thought 'this may kill me but they're so great I have to do it'." Hamilton took them under her wing and gave them a crash course in music-biz dos and don'ts – and though she and the Gunners later fell out (she sued them for money she'd allegedly invested in them), her role was clearly vital enough for Geffen to give her a staff job once they'd signed the band.

The pack of record companies in full cry represented a full stomach to five hungry musicians – and true to form, they hit them for as many square meals as they could muster. "We made them all take us out for dinner for a week or two and we started eating *good*," recalls Izzy. "We'd order all this food and drink, and say 'Okay, *talk!*'."

On March 26 1986, the band kissed poverty goodbye forever when they finally signed with Geffen. "You're the loudest band I've ever seen in my life," said one record company executive admiringly. Another was not quite as unrestrained with his praise. "Guns N'Roses?" he queried. "Yeah, they'll make it . . . if they live long enough."

Closeted in the luxury of a fully equipped professional studio for the first time, the band were introduced to producer Mike (Ozzy Osbourne, Survivor) Clink, their guide to this awesome new high-tech world. And 'Appetite For Destruction', released in July 1987, was the result – an album that combined the raw power of heavy metal with the anger and energy of punk in a unique way.

The angry, aggressive lyrics – totally 'in your face', as the expression goes – were as remarkable as the fiery musical backing that seared eardrums from San Francisco to Seattle. The sentiments came from the singer himself: given G N'R's controversial stance, no-one could possibly put words into Axl Rose's mouth. And those lyrics so often came from experience . . . *bitter* experience.

Take 'Out Ta Get Me', for instance – inspired, admits the writer, by spells in Indiana's many jail and correction homes. 'Rocket Queen' was based on a former girlfriend "alive . . . but there's not much left." More happily, 'Sweet Child O' Mine', "the first positive love song I've ever written", was inspired by model girl Erin Everly, soon to become Mrs Axl Rose.

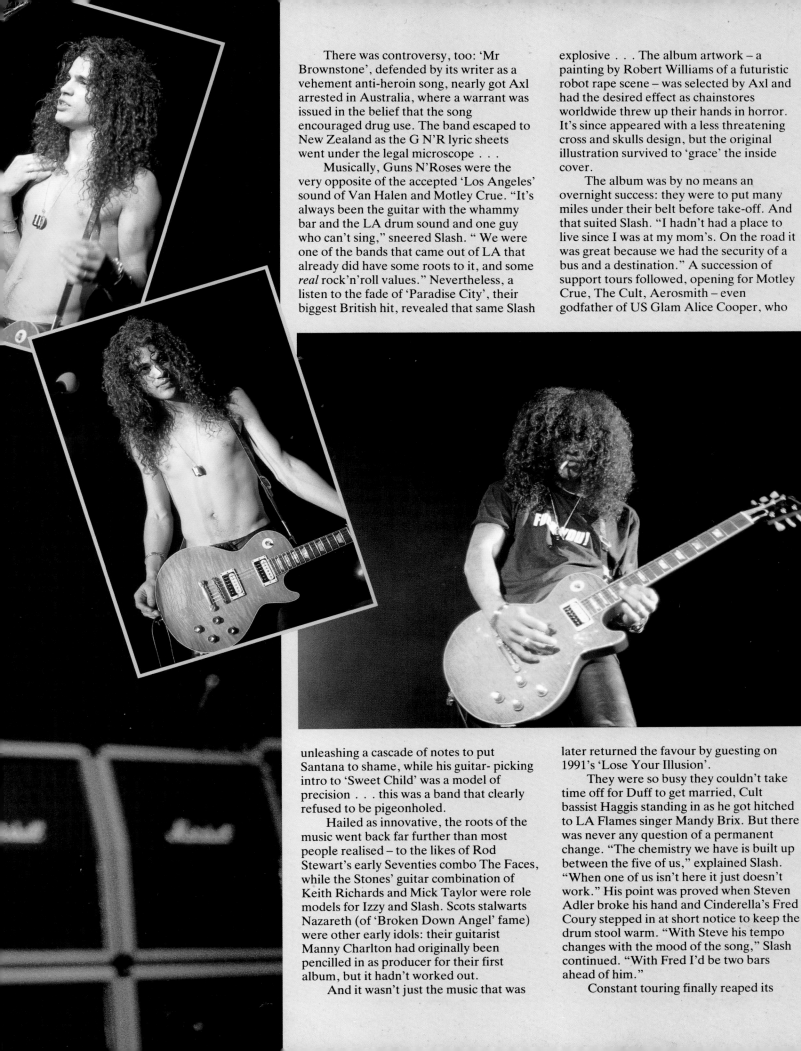

There was controversy, too: 'Mr Brownstone', defended by its writer as a vehement anti-heroin song, nearly got Axl arrested in Australia, where a warrant was issued in the belief that the song encouraged drug use. The band escaped to New Zealand as the G N'R lyric sheets went under the legal microscope . . .

Musically, Guns N'Roses were the very opposite of the accepted 'Los Angeles' sound of Van Halen and Motley Crue. "It's always been the guitar with the whammy bar and the LA drum sound and one guy who can't sing," sneered Slash. " We were one of the bands that came out of LA that already did have some roots to it, and some *real* rock'n'roll values." Nevertheless, a listen to the fade of 'Paradise City', their biggest British hit, revealed that same Slash

explosive . . . The album artwork – a painting by Robert Williams of a futuristic robot rape scene – was selected by Axl and had the desired effect as chainstores worldwide threw up their hands in horror. It's since appeared with a less threatening cross and skulls design, but the original illustration survived to 'grace' the inside cover.

The album was by no means an overnight success: they were to put many miles under their belt before take-off. And that suited Slash. "I hadn't had a place to live since I was at my mom's. On the road it was great because we had the security of a bus and a destination." A succession of support tours followed, opening for Motley Crue, The Cult, Aerosmith – even godfather of US Glam Alice Cooper, who

unleashing a cascade of notes to put Santana to shame, while his guitar- picking intro to 'Sweet Child' was a model of precision . . . this was a band that clearly refused to be pigeonholed.

Hailed as innovative, the roots of the music went back far further than most people realised – to the likes of Rod Stewart's early Seventies combo The Faces, while the Stones' guitar combination of Keith Richards and Mick Taylor were role models for Izzy and Slash. Scots stalwarts Nazareth (of 'Broken Down Angel' fame) were other early idols: their guitarist Manny Charlton had originally been pencilled in as producer for their first album, but it hadn't worked out.

And it wasn't just the music that was

later returned the favour by guesting on 1991's 'Lose Your Illusion'.

They were so busy they couldn't take time off for Duff to get married, Cult bassist Haggis standing in as he got hitched to LA Flames singer Mandy Brix. But there was never any question of a permanent change. "The chemistry we have is built up between the five of us," explained Slash. "When one of us isn't here it just doesn't work." His point was proved when Steven Adler broke his hand and Cinderella's Fred Coury stepped in at short notice to keep the drum stool warm. "With Steve his tempo changes with the mood of the song," Slash continued. "With Fred I'd be two bars ahead of him."

Constant touring finally reaped its

reward . . . and when 'Appetite For Destruction' topped the US charts in the summer of 1988, it had taken a full 50 weeks to get to the top. Meanwhile, their third single, 'Sweet Child O' Mine', equalled that impact – and made Guns N'Roses only the fifth hard-rock band in the history of the charts to score a US Number 1 after Bon Jovi (1986), Survivor (1982) and two others. 'Appetite' was only the second heavy metal debut album ever to top the US charts, Quiet Riot's 'Metal Health' being the first in January 1983.

Such success clearly came as a shock to the famous five. "It was never my idea to make it by joining a commercial band," said Duff. "And in fact 'Appetite' is not a commercial record. Its appeal has amazed me."

Suddenly, *everyone* wanted to know them – and when 'Welcome To The Jungle' was plucked to appear in the soundtrack to a Clint Eastwood movie, it looked like they were on their way to Hollywood! Izzy Duff and Slash all made cameo appearances – as, of all things, a rock band shooting a rock

video – but Slash confessed it was hardly a great career move. "It was a horrible movie . . . we thought it would be cool."

If films proved less than glamorous, the band's approach to videos was typically direct and down to earth. Kicking freaks, facepaint and floozies well and truly into touch, they concentrated on what they do best – full-throttle rock. Video direction was by Nigel Dick, for many years one of the brains behind Stiff Records – and while the only connection between Guns N'Roses and Madness was a certain insanity, the combination carried off the 1988 MTV award for Heavy Metal Video of the Year with the promo for 'Sweet Child'.

Britain took a little longer to appreciate the Guns N'Roses phenomenon. The first UK single, 'It's So Easy', didn't exactly set the charts alight – but the word was spreading at street level. Three sold-out nights at London's Marquee club in October 1987 were recorded and tracks released as B-side/12-inch bonuses.

Ten months later, the invitation to open the show at Donington's Monsters of Rock festival in August 1988 recognised that world domination was only a matter of time. But the death of two fans during GNR's set at Castle Donington was the culmination of a disastrous day when the heavens opened and giant video screens toppled over. Though the band initially played on unawares, two youths were crushed to death as 'It's So Easy' thundered from the speaker stacks. And in shades of The Rolling Stones' fatal Altamont appearance in 1969 when a member of the audience was stabbed to death in front of the cameras, the tragedy was captured on video by the band's road crew.

When quizzed earlier about their attitudes and responsibilities, the band had expressed the view that the danger inherent in their music was a part of their appeal. "I guess we are playing with fire," Duff had admitted. "I would seriously hate for anything to happen but we're not the kind of guys to really change our ways." Slash agreed. "Not to say that I condone crowd violence and riots, but it's part of the energy that we put out."

After Donington, Axl was regretful but essentially unrepentant. "I don't know really what to think about it. We didn't tell people to smash each other. We didn't tell people 'Drink so much alcohol that you can't f***ing stand up.' I don't feel responsible in those ways."

All was not roses . . . and commercial pressures too were rearing their heads. A year and a half had passed since 'Appetite', twelve months in which the band had covered every mile of road from New York to Los Angeles via Europe and Japan. It was clearly too soon for a live album – and the answer was ingenious indeed. 'G N'R Lies' was quite literally a half and half

album – the four tracks from 'Suicide' being balanced by four new songs to keep the fans happy. And with only 25,000 copies of 'Suicide' on the streets, it stopped a fair few life savings from going to the wall.

Four new songs? Make that three and a half . . . : 'You're Crazy', one of the first songs they wrote after inking the Geffen contract, had already been heard in rocked-up form on 'Appetite', but had been slowed back down to its original tempo. 'Patience', a hit single in waiting, and 'Used To Love Her' hadn't surfaced before in any shape or form – but it was the lyrically explicit 'One In A Million' that was to cause much controversy with its 'faggots' and 'niggers' references.

Clad in a fake tabloid newspaper sleeve as a riposte to the rumour mill, 'G N'R Lies' joined the six million-selling 'Appetite' in the racks in November 1988, making the band the first band in the Eighties to have two albums in the Top Five at the same time. Only The Beatles and four other acts had ever managed this. And by the time the single 'Patience' was released in June 1989, 'Lies' had already sold more than two million copies.

As well as the World's Most Dangerous Band, Guns N'Roses had now inherited the Bon Jovi mantle as the rock band to catch the imagination of the mass pop audience. And even though the fans had another album to tuck alongside 'Appetite', the classic debut just wouldn't lie down. 'Paradise City' hit Number 5 in the US charts in March 1989, reaching

Number 6 in Britain where the reissued 'Sweet Child' made the same position in May. Come June it was the turn of 'Lies' to be plundered for 45s as 'Patience' was unleashed to reach Number 4 in the US, Number 10 in the UK.

If Donington had marked the beginning of a backlash, October 1989 was the end of a troublesome year – and very nearly of the band itself. The Gunners had been booked to play a four-night series of concerts as special guests of The Rolling Stones at the Los Angeles Memorial Coliseum. It was a hometown gig, and the band were looking forward to blowing Jagger and Co off stage – but Axl was late arriving. And when he *did* arrive, what he found going on in the dressing room made him extremely reluctant to set foot on stage. After much persuasion by the management, he went on 15 minutes late to sing as if possessed – then stunned the capacity crowd by accusing certain members of the band of "Dancing with 'Mr Brownstone'," a clear reference to the first album's anti-heroin anthem of that name. This would, Axl insisted, be his very last gig with Guns N'Roses.

The following night, Slash averted the inevitable with a public promise from the Coliseum stage to clean up and sort his own personal problems out. It wasn't the first time Axl had parted company with the band: a no-show at Phoenix 18 months earlier had seen him sacked, then reinstated.

The press, inevitably, had a field day – but this was a band destined to be forever in the headlines . . . In Atlanta, Axl was arrested between numbers for attacking a security guard: the band completed their 45-minute set with assistance from a roadie and 15-minute solo spots from Slash and Steve. Axl pleaded guilty to avoid a trial. In Philadelphia, a pre-gig fight in a car park saw Axl locked up again: this time, persuasion from tour manager Doug Goldstein got him out without charge. In Chicago a businessman who called Axl a "Bon Jovi lookalike" started a brawl that took dozens of cops to break up and saw Axl and Steve renew their acquaintance with the slammer.

Izzy had his moments, too – not least in Hamburg, where he and Duff tied up the drummer of support act Faster Pussycat and put him in a lift. At the MTV Awards in 1989, he scrapped with Motley Crue singer Vince Neil, whose wife accused him of coming on strong . . . then was soon back in trouble for relieving himself in the aisle of an airliner. Axl, meanwhile, got involved in a backstage fight with British glam-rockers Dogs D'Amour at a Los Angeles club, while Duff was duffed up by a nightclub bouncer in New Orleans – but returned with 11 of his friends to right the wrong.

If clubland was out of bounds, Axl's home life was no better. He'd already complained of mistreatment by two policemen investigating loud music at his apartment when he was arrested in October 1990 after a neighbour accused him of breaking a bottle on her head. The case was dismissed, but Axl and Erin Everly, who'd married in April, parted just months afterwards.

Axl had made many emotional performances in his time – but none more dramatic than in a Reno, Nevada courtroom in February 1991 when his marriage was annulled. Confessing it "the biggest mistake of my life", he continued "We only spent two months together. She was always staying with friends. I just don't think she had any idea how to be a wife – or any desire to be, for that matter."

In happier times, he'd compared his relationship with Erin, daughter of Everly Brother Don, with that of Jim Morrison and Pamela Courson: "always fighting, but they were soulmates." You didn't have to be young, free and single to be a Gunner – but it clearly helped! Steven and Duff were hitched, but the band was clearly quite a rival for even the most dedicated wife to deal with.

Guns N'Roses had fired their opening musical salvo of 1990 in April with a three-song blast at the Farm Aid lll charity show in Indianapolis. Opening with 'Welcome To The Jungle' and the brand new 'Civil War', the showstopping finale was, appropriately, 'Down On The Farm' – written by British punks the UK Subs.

Their only releases of the year both appeared relatively anonymously as tracks on 'various artists' albums. Not that there was anything wrong with the music . . . A studio take of 'Knockin' On Heaven's Door', an audience favourite of the live show, adorned the mega-hit 'Days Of Thunder' soundtrack, while the aforementioned 'Civil War' was the band's gift to George Harrison when the former Beatle put together a charity fund-raising album for Romanian orphans called 'Nobody's Child'. Typically, the press chose not to headline this piece of G N'R generosity.

The big news of 1990 was the shock departure of drummer Steven Adler in July – amazingly the band's first personnel change since 1985. "His chops were all over the place," remarked Slash of his long-time friend, whose drug problem was affecting his playing. "And he was lying to us (about cleaning up). I was trying to talk sense into him but it never happened . . . and Axl and Duff had had it."

With their record label screaming yet again for a new album, a replacement was clearly needed – and *fast*! Adam Maples from The Sea Hags "didn't have the right vibe" for Slash, and while The Pretenders' Martin Chambers briefly filled in, the eventual choice was Matt Sorum from The Cult.

He joined keyboardist Dizzy Reed as a permanent member, and both new Gunners took their bow on 18 January 1991 – not, as might be expected, at some low-key club date, but at Brazil's internationally-televised Rock in Rio Festival in the massive Maracana stadium.

Anybody expecting an over-rehearsed performance was cruelly disappointed. When Dizzy Reed wasn't playing keyboards, for instance, Axl insisted he contributed percussion – even on numbers he'd never played on before! In the guitar department, Slash and Izzy were cranking out earbending leads and riffs as if they'd never been away: Matt Sorum provided an earthshaking foundation on which Duff could build his distinctive loping bass runs, while Axl stalked the stage like a lion on heat. They even dared to tease with a trio of new numbers: 'All Tied Up', a great set opener, 'Double Talkin' Jive' and the funky 'Bad Apples', while 'Estranged' was the meat in the sandwich of a triple-punch encore featuring 'Sweet Child' and 'Rocket

Queen' to end a show a towel-swathed Axl backstage acclaimed as "the best show we've *ever* done".

This stunning performance confirmed that the Gunners were still blazing away with both barrels – but critics were quick to point out that on vinyl the evidence still amounted to just but one and a half albums. What the world was waiting for was a new LP. For many months, the world had a name – 'Use Your Illusion', after a painting Axl had chosen – but not a hint of a release date.

On January 13, 1991 – a Sunday, not a Friday, incidentally – they entered the familiar confines of Los Angeles' Rumbo Studios with Mike Clink again at the controls. It was clear that things were happening – then suddenly came the news that with 36 songs in the can, with a likely release date of April, the problem now was which songs to choose!

The appointed month came and went, but the sudden summoning of king remixer Bill (Sex Pistols, Pretenders) Price suggested a glimmer of light at the end of

the tunnel. Even though Slash had insisted there were no singles (because each and every track contained at least one swear word), 'Don't Cry' appeared in June as the first single – and predictably proved a chart success. Guns N'Roses were back!

'Use Your Illusion' finally made it in July as what the music business claimed was a 'formatting first' – two double albums in wide-spine single sleeves. The music was every bit as original as the packaging with saxophones, mandolins, keyboards and even an Indian sitar floating in the mix. Slash described the release as "Very self-indulgent . . . it might take people aback a bit." So what was new?

'Use Your Illusion' contained epics a-plenty, notably 'November Rain' and the anti-drug 'Coma' – both 10 minutes plus. Other likely candidates for final track selection included the Stones-y 'Dust And Bones', the punky 'Shotgun Blues', and 'The Garden', featuring Axl harmonising with Alice Cooper. Other titles included 'Why Do You Look At Me (When You Hate Me)', 'Locomotive', 'Don't Damn Me', '14 Years', 'You Ain't The First' and 'So Fine'.

The announcement of 'Use Your Illusion' and the world tour that accompanied it stirred the rock'n'roll world as never before. No stone was left unturned – *everyone* wanted to see the show. The band's first scheduled British date at London's Wembley Stadium in August sold an unprecedented 47,000 tickets on the first day of sale, while a live album was already being pencilled in for release at the end of the tour to add to sales of nine million for 'Appetite' and three and a quarter million for 'G N'R Lies'.

Everything had come right for Slash, who'd spent his year off playing with every big name from Dylan to Michael Jackson, Iggy Pop to Lenny Kravitz. But far from becoming the star axe-slinger on the session scene, he clearly appreciated Guns N'Roses' unique chemistry as much as anyone. "If it weren't for Axl I could still be searching for a singer," he pointed out. As for the future, his diagnosis was refreshingly optimistic. "To go from nowhere to here was such a huge mind trip. Now that it's happened, and we've managed to keep it together, I don't think we'll go through that kind of shock again."

Izzy, too, was happy to be back in the engine room of rock's biggest live attraction. "Is there life after Guns N'Roses?" he quipped. "We'll die too early for that. When the band dies I die too."

As ever, Axl has the last word on the future of the rock phenomenon that bears his name. "I'm not going to say we'll be around forever – but I hope I'll write the kind of music that sticks around for a long time."

No problem!

GUNS N'ROSES DISCOGRAPHY

UK LPs

APPETITE FOR DESTRUCTION
Geffen WX125 (August '87)

APPETITE FOR DESTRUCTION
Geffen WX125W ('88, Limited w/stickers)

G N'R LIES
Geffen WX218 (December '88)

G N'R LIES
Geffen WX218W ('88, Limited w/stickers)

USE YOUR ILLUSION I
(Release scheduled July '91)

USE YOUR ILLUSION II
(Release scheduled July '91)

UK CDs

APPETITE FOR DESTRUCTION
Geffen 9241482 (December '87)

G N'R LIES
Geffen 9241982 ('88)

GUNS N'ROSES
Baktabak CBAK4015 (Nov '89, interview compact disc)

USE YOUR ILLUSION I
(Release scheduled July '91)

USE YOUR ILLUSION II
(Release scheduled July '91)

UK SINGLES

IT'S SO EASY/MR BROWNSTONE
Geffen GEF22 (June '87)

WELCOME TO THE JUNGLE/WHOLE LOTTA ROSIE
Geffen GEF30 (September '87)

SWEET CHILD O'MINE/OUT TA GET ME
Geffen GEF43 (Aug '88)

WELCOME TO THE JUNGLE/NIGHTRAIN
(re-release)
Geffen GEF47 (October '88)

PARADISE CITY/I USED TO LOVE HER
Geffen GEF50 (March '89)

SWEET CHILD O'MINE/OUT TA GET ME (re-release)
Geffen GEF55 (May '89)

PATIENCE/ROCKET QUEEN
Geffen GEF56 (May '89)

NIGHTRAIN/RECKLESS LIFE
Geffen GEF60 (Aug '89)

DON'T CRY/TITLE TO BE CONFIRMED
(Release scheduled June '90)

UK 12"

IT'S SO EASY/MR BROWNSTONE/SHADOW OF YOUR LOVE/MOVE TO THE CITY
Geffen GEF22T (June '87)

IT'S SO EASY/MR BROWNSTONE/SHADOW OF YOUR LOVE/MOVE TO THE CITY
Geffen GEF22TP (June '87, pic disc)

WELCOME TO THE JUNGLE/WHOLE LOTTA ROSIE/IT'S SO EASY/KNOCKIN' ON HEAVEN'S DOOR
Geffen GEF30T (September '87)

WELCOME TO THE JUNGLE/WHOLE LOTTA ROSIE/IT'S SO EASY/KNOCKIN' ON HEAVEN'S DOOR
Geffen GEF30TW (September '87, w/poster sleeve)

WELCOME TO THE JUNGLE/WHOLE LOTTA ROSIE/IT'S SO EASY/KNOCKIN' ON HEAVEN'S DOOR
Geffen GEF30TP (September '87, pic disc)

SWEET CHILD O'MINE/OUT TA GET ME/ROCKET QUEEN
Geffen GEF43T (August '88)

SWEET CHILD O'MINE/OUT TA GET ME/ROCKET QUEEN
Geffen GEF43TV (August '88, in special sleeve)

WELCOME TO THE JUNGLE/NIGHTRAIN/YOU'RE CRAZY (re-release)
Geffen GEF47T (October '88)

WELCOME TO THE JUNGLE/NIGHTRAIN/YOU'RE CRAZY (re-release)
Geffen GEF47TW (October '88, poster sleeve)

WELCOME TO THE JUNGLE/NIGHTRAIN/YOU'RE CRAZY (re-release)
Geffen GEF47TV (October '88, w/patch)

WELCOME TO THE JUNGLE/NIGHTRAIN/YOU'RE CRAZY (re-release)
Geffen GEF47TP (October '88, pic disc)

PARADISE CITY/I USED TO LOVE HER/ANYTHING GOES
Geffen GEF50T (March '89)

SWEET CHILD O'MINE/OUT TA GET ME (re-release)
Geffen GEF55T (May '89)

PATIENCE/ROCKET QUEEN/W AXL ROSE INTERVIEW
Geffen GEF56T (May '89)

NIGHTRAIN/RECKLESS LIFE
Geffen GEF60T (Aug '89)

DON'T CRY/TITLE TO BE CONFIRMED
(Release scheduled June '91)

UK SPECIAL

GUNS N'ROSES INTERVIEW PICTURE DISC
Music & Media CT1013 (Dec '87)

GUNS N'ROSES INTERVIEW PICTURE DISC
Baktabak BAK2079 (Dec '87)

SWEET CHILD O'MINE/OUT TA GET ME/ROCKET QUEEN
Geffen GEF43TE (August '88, special sleeve, 10")

WELCOME TO THE JUNGLE/NIGHTRAIN/YOU'RE CRAZY (re-release)
Geffen GEF47CD (October '88, CD single)

GUN N'ROSES INTERVIEW PICTURE DISC COLLECTION
Baktabak BAKPAK1011 ('88, 7" Set)

PARADISE CITY/I USED TO LOVE HER/SWEET CHILD O'MINE
Geffen GEF50CD (March '89, CD single)

PARADISE CITY/I USED TO LOVE HER/ANYTHING GOES
Geffen 9275704 (April '89, cassingle)

PARADISE CITY/I USED TO LOVE HER
Geffen GEF50P (April '89, pic disc single; gun shaped)

PARADISE CITY/I USED TO LOVE HER
Geffen GEF50X (March '89, holster package)

APPETITE FOR CONVERSATION
Baktabak BAK6001 (Mar '89, interview picture disc LP)

SWEET CHILD O'MINE/OUT TA GET ME/MOVE TO THE CITY/IT'S SO EASY/WHOLE LOTTA ROSIE (re-release)
Geffen GEF55CD (May '89, CD single)

PATIENCE/ROCKET QUEEN
Geffen GEF56CD (May '89, CD single)

PATIENCE/ROCKET QUEEN
Geffen GEF56C (May '89, cassingle)

NIGHTRAIN/RECKLESS LIFE
Geffen GEF60CD (August '89, CD single)

NIGHTRAIN/RECKLESS LIFE
Geffen GEF60C (August '89, cassingle)